ECHO SYSTEM

ECHO SYSTEM

poems

JULIE AGOOS

The Sheep Meadow Press

Cover: River Series II, Panel D, Monoprint by Louise Kalin, 2014

Typeset by The Sheep Meadow Press

Distributed by The University Press of New England

Library of Congress Cataloging-in-Publication Data

Agoos, Julie, 1956-
[Poems. Selections]
Echo system : poems / Julie Agoos.
pages ; cm
ISBN 978-1-937679-56-9
I. Title.
PS3551.G59A6 2015
811'.54—dc23

All inquiries and permission requests should be addressed to the publisher:

The Sheep Meadow Press
PO Box 84
Rhinebeck, NY 12572

For Ella, Henri, Isaac, and for Jeremy

Contents

□ □ □

□ □ □

ECHO SYSTEM

These poems were made with the radio on, intermingling their news in the news of the world. I was thinking of the body laboring and giving birth, and of the mind adapting to age in an age of bombarding information: Biology of first and last, of news that will not stay news. The radio-speak like a first experience of words, an echoing of half-remembered lines of verse. For those echoes and their poems of origin I owe thanks to many, including Czeslaw Milosz, Robert Browning, Percy Bysshe Shelley, George Herbert, Robert Frost, Theodore Roethke, John Coltrane, James Merrill, Elizabeth Bishop, Alan Jay Lerner, Thomas Hardy, Billie Holiday, Robert Lowell, Walt Whitman, T.S. Eliot, W.B. Yeats. For the radio sojourn among voices equally subject to distortion and loss, I am indebted to many anonymous storytellers whose words, localized and sudden and rare, made up the bed of the echo system. From the sustaining life of the made: punctuated equilibrium; genotype and phenotype turned on their heads; found languages joining mine in time.

EXISTENTIAL CENSUS

Window   park   home . . .
Grocery   work   school . . .
Of ourselves
What we know is
Numberless stars
To be counted
Federal lifelong
What we know is
No for the yes
Steep fines and clauses
Constitutions required
More speech than I
In my cause confide
Reports undocumented
Jobs no job
What we know is Time
Is representative
By stoop by block
Where fires confine
Two feet in two worlds
By street to be known
In this meanwhile
Speak to be counted
If you're alive, that is
If you're entirely
Here, in this city . . .

GRACIAS A USTEDES

"At every cross street," one says, *"like birds in flames,*
Bright vests going down to the sea.

And miles and miles of City Parks at dusk.
And wet-backed, on their knees, all spannered and trowelled—

I thought the sky was in blossom! Blooms
10 lights and the bridge."

"As inconceivable to me,
That water and light and today too late—

There's no one coming for us," one nods,
"Such knowledge wasting such green life—

These coastal floods," she adds, "January
5, 1813 – or '38, I mean, I can't

Remember which Advisory was which:
'Brittany Under Siege, 1909'?

Or was it 'Girl With Trident, 2010'?"
"It rained for days then, didn't it?

And Tokyo's blood-red flag let down
Its rainbow sign of static,

All reporting fever of sorts
For miles and miles of radioactive City—

All going down to the sea!"
"And yet the Met got on the plane I read

Despite the water-shedding
("*Wet-backed, on their knees!*")

— As for the rest, each posed
His claim: Oh please God no more

Fire, but flowers next time
(Love is best)!"

COLD WAR FREE RADIO

I say Wilcox
On your side of the pond
The deer have free run of the park
Or that's the way it was then what

Not so anymore dear Burke that fence
Runs now like a net
The deer fight tooth and claw
To get over over here

Ha ha the skies extending what are they still
Grey and wet and green cool grass
Yet crowded in fog as was or have such
Things then heated up there since

By God things are stark yes enough
And ever in contrast to what they were last
As no one knows better of course than yourself of which
To whom we oversold that old script once

Come come there must be at least some proxy law
To thaw one's ancient cargo in as then I'd bet
It's a mindwarp in truth in fact at best
That nothing remains at all of that time at all

But the station clock and the chalice cross
And the pith helmet and the oxygen tank
And the jelly spoon and the box of milk
And the yellow grey mustard tin

And the musterfields croaking with frogs, ha ha . . .

STIMULUS

O dew-cold road
The fugitive's on the lam

Thou grant a conference room
To flush or finish him

On-off a conference phone
On off on hold to hold him

Mount of Olympic City's
Billion-fold made strong

By glint of manual work
—Gold leaf low-hanging hawks

On the wind
O Radio

...That this is not the judgment hour
For some of them's a blessed thing...

Sun's low-grade payload
Of news at 6 a.m.

Swept in on the maps
...Fortune's teller...Banks

Clouds...   Mild windfall...
Theatre hours

When cats drag in
Cold chestnuts old cash

As tyrannous dogs out track
The crumbling catwalks

State Police cars shaking loose
Their radar of coolant and Skoals

Black tarmac scored
Where two roads met

A mess spreads out but not
Un-controllable — O Thou!

Whose credit provided
Barge to seawall

Here where cranes replace
The balustrades   A chorus

Drowns in oil: All's business
Underfoot: All's fair

In unison: Against
The shore complaints

Come camouflaged in prayer:
Oh Who Oh Thou

Will buy this
Wonderful morning?

CASH FOR CLUNKERS

What I mean is
What I hoped was

At that time
Then I believed

To sleep summer nights
As the dreaming said

Oh help me get past
Oh God what I meant's

I chose accounts empty
On no account yet

If only my health
If only the Bill had —

Residents said yet
Worried that Congress

What if I still
My God a Tsunami

Paid on the nose
Once reason went

If it's not one thing
Now the recess starting

Residents said if
Worried well Congress

Dream a little dream
You'll want for nothing

Once understanding's
No object surely

Vote with your head
Whatever is asked

This barcode barrage
I'm in I mean

Take it from me —
A pound on the penny

All in a day's one
Planet among money

A penny ante
Among many

IN LABOR

Wake up freedom
From walking upright from thought

Alone on a bed soft air is brightening
Closed one eye sun's retinal expanse

Seeing but in no rush to the idea
Age-old story stars to circumstance

Among flowers now petals wet bare soft
Of the neighbor cats biocellate

Chattering uphill low gear temperature
No planting bent to the dirt-armed pods'

Wide casements cracked biographers
Of a man dancing backwards upward past

As if one had tuned him louder static song
Night-driven fruit fresh ages underfoot

Descendant strain of pooled survivors massed
To water now milk to warm first cause

Ghost volunteers none real none crests
No fast breeched foot jeweled fontanelle emerge

Through green clockhands reading seconds out
In real-time bandwidth off hours exhaled

Far moon car lights gravel churning dust
To chrome upriver slowly withdrawn

As ghosts to the table sung and closer come
The nightclerk's spreadsheets in their phylum soon

Then books then racks of magazines recycle
Birds too far farsighted to hear beyond

My ear alone repeating scolding sounds
Of blood's tremulous pleaders upside down

Till there on the birthing branch a flower
Dawn-created whistles scattering gold

A warm/cold gratitude as once a pulse
Had happened long all morning with a force

That broke down arms distilled in sweat
And thoughts full/empty spurning flesh

To lave the child before the child is born
And lift from heaviness her very own

Lingering long surreal of solitude
Dry/wet of Ocean inside a shell

An irreal meeting coming quick to form
Her concentration that in stealing on

This cosmos more or less breaks open
Oblivion then hands unhanding her

Her will — life — unfurled — *she* commands
You now: *Lift her out mother fetch me to her*

FEED-FIELD, FEED-FUEL, & THE CHINESE MEAT-EATERS

Hunger understands understatement
A rolling pin for pain champagne
Over the bow out for now—

Hardly had the thing been explained
Than a billion more clapped
Spoon to the bowl

Euphrates drying up:
"A real thirst in Iraq"
The Minister of Planning said —

7 dams downstream from Syria
Markets rose in barley date-palm
Citrus in the Baghdad stadium

— Who'd take a life in giving one
What's mine is yours Child
I am yours *am* you

But of grain I have none
From fields where lowing herds put the heat on
7 dams downstream from Turkey

We don't mean to but we do
Heat things up — off
To the hospitals to be born

While moons above the combines strike
The barns and dark clouds suck
And suck until you scream for less

CARDINAL

Crying
Alarmed

Tree
Felling

Spruce
House

Despoiled
Disarmed

*

Refuged
Sun

High
Strung

Beaded
Red

Six-
Sided

*

Cheekturned
Unlocked

Sky
Spars

*

Hedge
Crest

Spilling
Words

Hoarded
Fusillade

*

Jailed
Spring's

Daughter
Targeted

COME IN AND PUT YOUR BAG DOWN

stage directions for birth

Enter stage left a body   *Night*
Babe now in arms now full
Face front and enter again
And enter again   Now right
Stage blocked spots lengthen
Night body tall   *All bones*
Scrim similar *what then was shadow*
All's changed that was then
Nor yet where you now I will

Write speechless as directed once
Write infantile squalled   Full
Staged voice timeless as directed
Now I am this bit that same
Stage-crafted body tireless
I now my own am yours as you extend
Surpassing time tall tales as when
From wings time or timelessness
Those stars (exeunt) ever arranged

This clear blackdrop rearranged
Full house this depth appears no less
Bottomless November mid
November all at words less one mouth
Speechlost timeless month mild between us
Whispered to the next one ear to hear with *(and applause)*

—for Mort Rosenthal

EVE

In one hand an apple
In the other a pencil
Lightning flash of the left/right brain

The salt and pepper as compatible
Yet on cloudy days the white grains
Inflate inflect the black to blue specks

Elsewhere on its horizon a name incurs
From under the mind's obsessed inspection
Homeostatic occurs in each red cell

Which as she writes it down still vanishes
A thousand thousand years impressed in carbon
Tearing up the looseleaf biosphere

Where gradual yellow candlelight's
Lengthening just catches sight of her
Globed against the surface of the moon

As over and over again in Genesis
The sheen where a mother's thumb had pressed
A fruitful brazen justice taking hold

RADIO THEORY OF MIND

These are thy wondres lord of power,
Bringing down to hell or up to heaven in an hour
Making a chiming of a passing bell.
                    — *George Herbert*

With each passing hour
A change. To observe
Is to limit potential states
But from this rolling earth to hear

Is to multiply: The *particules*
Transporting their accounts a shadow-
Noise of worlds in a spread of light
Invisible waves that signal-shower

Far beyond distinguishable loci
Desert places between stars on stars
Where inextinguishable otherwise
Our intimate hypothetical eye

Of the storm engraving the Real
Repeats itself — or is it the other way 'round?
The brain's magic terrifies
As twinned towers raised on a word

Whose each cell occupies a cause
And swells to life   *Turn it off!*
But I can't Montaigne
You see I — well —

I object myself between
This poem and that voice
Whose word were all if I could spelle
And all words amplify

SUB-ROUTINE

The intricate details, the drives you take for granted

What's popularly thought of as

Free will of course

When your biology changes

As evidence demonstrates

There are limits and further examples

The assumption of chance or choice

The lesson is reinforced

The limits of will

I'm that/I'm this

By the pendulum drop't

An other/or another one

On what I thought I was

And then returned to this time being

Outside absent the norm

Until eccentric beside the point

Or else depending

Where one starts one's story from

A niche ex-temporized

As hand in hand

Through Eden took one's solitary course

Survival's artifice at once

Selected for which was

A going forth

In undetected compromise

THE STORY WAS ALL-CONSUMING

Anonymous people led by daylight
Past hedges into the zooming City
Everything looming in triplicate or tens
Phones and meters . . . ambulances . . .
As if an allegory were being penned
And nothing else were true but this
That kingdom sundered like a truck by landmines
Rescued sticks on a woodsman's back
Before the dreadful symbolizing psalmed:
Each stick a voice each voicing its refusal
That all need not be lost again
On soil returned to battle-crops
Pick-up sticks whose orders over *alles*
Transformed the geo-genetic drift to soy
A little self-serving it's true but still
Recoiled from being bound in a drowse like them
Of the body politic she'd heard it said
(As her thinking took her anywhere else):
Today it's impossible! All image no sound!
We *had thought-balloons* we *had nightly broadcasts*
We played jazz riffs on what we read
And whatever we'd hear of life that's what led
From all those archetypes and the static hoax
To rescue of the social body harmed —
I would still rather take my wars cold!

RUSSIAN? NO, HE'S STALLIN'

How close are the mouth and eye
Involuntary bath of fire
I laughed until I cried or the reverse
Each turn on History's turnpike tapped
A reflex somewhere in the visual cortex
Wherever I'm most blind to the state of war —
Still what I hear is a rhythm over the steppes . . .

If this were the last encounter with reference
If a scantron were your only choice
Mouth sewn shut by a distracting rule
A volley of school years rushing past
And the dirty wars in the middle years
Full of dark secrets you had only to guess at
And earn your 200 points on the raw
All for writing your name on the scale to play
Would you pay on the loan of those years again?

Be careful whose interest you pray to or wish for
Lest you live to be baptized in a different faith
Or die to be swept eternally off
Or onto consumer lists kept up
By the holy three who got out alive
Those natural phenoms literalized
Or sometimes evanesced or do I mean apotheosized
Depending on the quickest route the reflex takes

As mosses green at the root spring up
Then die back for their progress over the lawn
Or sometimes grey to monuments
Sticks in a frieze to throw an Albert Speer at —

You want it to matter what tears convey
A genuine feel for things that can't be named
And want the laughter to be as quick
As coal compressed and appreciated
Resource vesting the deep heart's *cuore*
Fear in flight *toward* the tangible pulse not away
(That another might look on it and someday write
And ledgers grow thick that began despite
Time waiting for no man, etc., etc.)
— The 25 million allied in time with tides
— All there is all there in the books
Still to be read when none pass by on horses

PROMENADE

At some point the city said:
You lamp-lighters will be the sun-
Makers, drop a fake acoustic
Ceiling down on six o'clock
Winter summer on the pilasters,
The need to succumb to Power like that
Shaken over the living room rugs the city walls

Who's in who's out of the pattern?

Father's the word most spoken now
Whether or not one resides at home
Lowering sun at a cost of stars
And a starless outer world on my child

What will I tell her? — No home
But the atom bombardment
Running in Time's far glass
Where dream and night attest their code
To the ferris wheel of the chromosomes;
And the Promenade rushing on and on;
The landmarks wet
With a love supreme?

THE BARRIER OF SKIN

The eyes can't look away
Such staring falsifies
A bandwidth of ambivalence
As the horse at a canter rears
The steeple chase is splintered
Out millions a silk purse torn
Blood filling the ear like fog
Its twin strange to say
Shuddering winces
As love though it end in tears
Clarifies those who entered
Transformed by the ambulance horns
Waves years and years
A cut in time each stitch
The nuns at their prayers
The doc at his CT scanner
And the journalists oh yes
Under sun yellow as fever
Above the Mediterranean
Where I twice lost my life

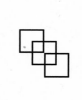

READING OF LEBANON

The street now no entry
And tapered by rubble.
A sidewalk unpacked.
The schoolyard all inventory,

500 chairs in the sun
And miles of linoleum flooring
Flecked by mortar; 500
Polished desks in open air.

3 o'clock: eclipse
Of bells, a glitter of prayer
Through the hi-tech network
Of shells (wherever

Legible), of windows
And doors still chalked
On the skeletal abstract
Of classrooms and halls.

Oh Strict and Familiar Mother
Of Seasons such light
Scores the boards
With the ropes to be learned in the ceasefire there

Between three and dinner!

FLU SHOT

We were waiting for a pandemic
Imprint of versus first come first serve
As when gradation not dichotomy
Arising from within each thing or form
Adapts each to its natural purposes

So in the meantime we took drugs to tend
And alleviate fear of fear of the pandemic
Research suggesting a marriage of strains is best
Symptoms decades apart still vigorous
Recurrent now in populations such
As cover enough among us globally
To keep the project purposed and ongoing

Research suggesting a thriving viral load
Supports a thriving funding as some now claim
Disease to be mere invention of the CEO's
Two paths surviving in a yellow mood
Driving home our highly paranoid style
As way leads on to way one knows one would
Survive these cognitive frames and processes
Otherwise directed to no end
At least in one's own self-prophecy

But in truth it's the other way round and the CEO's
Are invented by the disease the competent kind
That burrows into a cell which side it's on
Or what futures will tell completely foreclosed

My face in its fixtures too by which I mean
Not the visible figures of eyes and mouth
But the rictus of words in their skeletal narrative
That deeper darkness of the snow's approach
That in the available nuclear language appalls

— I know it sounds paranoid but mentalities
Fundamental to herds make true
That everything flows and we are passing through
(Beyond the stars to leverage now)
On a river all underground foretold to last
Just to the sell-by date stamped in the fold
— Tattoo of a fixed world of unlimited fixes

READING THE GREAT WAR

Clocks and carpets and chairs
On the lawn all day,
And brightest things that are theirs...
—Thomas Hardy

So much rain there can be no auction,
No emptying like the emptying of the rain
Through hemlock, beech, and oak and to the grass
Days on end, outwitting gain.

So much gray there can be no loss
Of matter—gray holding the mortared ground together
And everything that ever happened here
Remembered by the weather.

Day or night? he asks. His body says
He is growing tired. But he knows to stay awake
One more hour. For years he bends
Over the page pleasure saves –

Where all the household objects that are theirs,
Despite the years when neither hand nor eye
Dared make a sign, answer her –
As when the sun shines, some days.

BICYCLE

Spoke of how the wall
Ray and shadow
And ice twice fell
And balls rolled

Of a boxspring
And a wheelbearing
Axle assembly
Boot and shaft

Rust contacts once
Supplied by cable
Disc-mount notched
Numerical

Of chain mail
That rattled alarm
Sprung gear boxed
A back-up signal

To someone caught out
At a celebration
Past curfew of bells
Separate events

So you can't get out
But you can't get in
The pins the cams
Interlocked

All a free-for-all
Of a low-grade drop

In a degraded code
Leaked oil transmits

To the key patrol
Of a line supplied
In a Frankfurt cell
That was news

SATIRES OF CIRCUMSTANCE

Can it be you that I hear?
            —Thomas Hardy

i. *In a trench*

In case I was killed
What actually took place
For my family's sake — well —

Significant events—brace
Yourself—get the tape rolling—
Recording whatever actually took place

You never want to go through spoiling
For the first attack —
Train as you go — a toiling —

Of course it's like catching a break
Off a wave, the louder
It gets the less you feel it shake

The nerves some events in a crowd
Bring on that never took place;
The real thing keeps running aground.

In a dream: who first ran over took days —
I don't see who he was —
My dreams blur the facts between them and us —

Just a spot of time spent on my ass
An immense drone of fear
Then more like elation after the blast

That they died and you're here
Still making out
You're alive and whatever else they were

'S the starfire now of a total rout
In a dune in the dark you're alive
There's nothing more than that to get

Ten will get you a full five
To lie down flat
Go on record again—your wife—

Should you die she'll have that—
Words what had taken your place
Your voice at least the voice of it

Not knowing's the worst thing there is
For a couple of years
The feeling resurfaces

Each time you dream what you wanted her to hear
She still hasn't listened –
Can't – the radio you share

Always in on/off position
A fugitive to your refugee
You go to again and again to listen

All on the same frequency—
1000s of them had given up—
If you could have heard the artillery

More than I care to now – pop-pop
—An adrenaline rush—
Pop overactive hell yeah hot me up

You'd have gotten clear of the tanks (hush-hush)
Of the right or wrong or indifferent
There in the burning bush

We could process all night hellbent
Armored in the less is more
When he said 'engage' and down they went—

It was murder it's murder all right but Sir
My views have changed quite a bit
Back then I said goddamn let them surrender

They were willing to pay it was written about
The public then
Was loud   They still feel guilt

I mean my men
Misunderstood
There was of course confusion

There's little good
To come of it now
Of course it's all one-sided

Myself? My views
Have changed
I can't say how

I struggle myself   A range
A rationale
Doesn't help   Some time ago I changed

ii. *In a nightclub mirror (on furlough)*

Lucille does
For him
What Somali
Princes do

First chance
He gets
To reflect
He genuflects

The more
You know: Silver
And myrrh
And frankincence

The more
Myself I am
The more I can
Address you

*

How can a man
See himself
When sell-out's
The game

No more
Nor less an art
Than turns this room
Into the mirror

Ad infinit —
So on etc.
And there but for you
Grace I go

*

This wet
Sky's stormy
Weather
I guess

Some steam's
Gonna fall
No constancy
In clouds

How can a man
Be *himself?* We do
Not mean to but
We do heat things up

We do not
Mean to but
We do indeed
Heat things up too

iii. *On a train*

Of an idea man's
Pure gold:
Diggy do that innovative

(Higher pitched
Bellow
Crowded arm rest)

40-minutes-for-hire
Radio show rail-
Interviews the quiet car

For the moment my doubt
In all honesty's
Stabbed in the back

To get a dollar's
Pure semantics
Listen you

I'm telling this tale!
(and I did)
All right? His

Audience kicked back
Still from the effects
When he prefaced it

Sad lists led to sadder
More background led
To naysayers all:

Not a hit with the ladies
Life's a remix, Dude!
Gather round you-all!

Mothers and sons
Dontcha know . . .
Producing pure messages

(His father's a medium barely
The feeling resurfaces each
New Year spent on his own)

The funniest thing was
—*You've got to hear this*—
Was far and above

Till the walls caved in
He'd prayed to be happy
In bed—*you don't*

Keep that just
To yourself—Should it all die
Down don't press erase

Diggy do you give gold!
In a strange way yes
He provoked a triumph

So far and above
His life fulfilled
Dare to believe this

Done unto others pure
Pride   *What a mess!*
Man, life's a railroad

Did he stay by the phone
When she visited next
In a strange way yes

Nonetheless it was just
To be happy
Her voice that was his vice

iv. *Operator*

Special effects
Can put you through
Same old same old
Speak now

Sounds different off
Hold it close
Let me try again
There speak now

Hi-tech recorded
No? Shall I try for you?
A coupon book a ratio-
N book of static

Sorry   press once
To speak   like that
Press once
To end the call yes

Interrupt
To cut him off
Delay's the thing
Then to speak

A kind of ration-
Ing   an inverse
Special effect
I've lost

Speak now
If I can I will
Reply in peace
Tomorrow then

Same time
Where I am not
Today's 6 hours ahead
Sometime again

v. *In a rowhouse garden (childhood)*

Stuck in time

Walled copper

Of stone gardens paved

Shadows crawling

Like snails under heatlamp

Silhouetted beertrace

Cracked bowl's surface

Upward in alleys that join

As each spills in slowmo

From its shell

And the streets

By no other mark

Distinguished extinguish

Not even by names

—St Paul's, N. Charles—

Industrious row houses

Uncle or aunt's for sale

On Calvert on the 9:18

From Chicago she said

Dinner's on the table

Or on me I forget

And the Bistro's not far

Like the *Pays* something

—In the Basque you know—

But hey nonetheless

A seventh wonder –

Out of the shell

Endlessly reeling

Barnacled copper

Senses a daisy wheel

In a hyped-up type

On a quarter inch thick

Of cardboard spelling

A dish in French

A five-course *prix fixe*

At the end of which

We have come to the city

A flea market limits

Beds of foreclosure

Mount finds like this

Each table-collage

Ripped from dark walls

Of industrial old world

Sheds where once

A salon met over snails

In the avant garde

Or the *après le deluge*

One *tableau vivant*

Lasting through September

August I meant

Caesar's wedge

In snow shoulder

Retracted by cold

That has coolly kept on

Repeating itself

In the spiral form

Of a round idea

In the same garden

Neither in nor out

A poor one at that

Neither consequence

Nor hold-out cause

In the signing world's push

An ambivalent bivalve

Still trumpeting its hold

When the pressure's on:

Exist   Exist

vi. *On a promenade*

Years back one ate
With a spoon

What was properly drunk
Through a straw

A stray taste
Was good news

Minds melded
The last dregs

What began well
Ended well

All on the house.
Now all on the promenade

Time carding
Wool over ice

A sound swallows itself
In an empty glass

A puck sinks in a well
At the end of days

Each counterweight
To the late night drone

Of a stranger who speaks
Straight from the crowd:

OUT WITH THE OLD!
The news on the street

Not as it was
In the sheer dark

All else a voice
Alone one might

Not otherwise believe
Awaits above

vii. *On a plane (re-up)*

Turn it off now
I'm about to leave
These Chinese ladies

Hopefully someday
They'll go on tour
What's mine is yours

At nighttime very quiet
In the day a lot of kids
Every eye seeks an ATM

A cell phone always rings
In my neighborhood
There's no release

Taking the place
Like a flight of sun
On vacation I couldn't breathe

The musical thought of words
I missed you so much
Pleasure leaves me dumb

My feelings g-
Force (it's a cliché
I think) some gravity

We'll be ok
We'll see each other more
The more I think

The more I'm where you are
Fine lines between
A lover or stalker

Goodbye is hard
Sounds so much like
A war going on

But the battle was over
10 minutes ago
10 minutes after

The plane went up
And Brownee Maghee
For a moment New York's

A hard horse to ride
I am so far
Out of my mind

viii. *At a desk*

Measure for measure   Bodies together
Their itinerary holds

See it's typed on an old Olivetti
Reading the strokes I

Remember almost the thinking making out
Of intent to go

His flight plan knowing it unlikely
How were we to know

A riot now to think how young they were
Entrained in rain

Scrambling tent to car or awake from a dream
Vividly prophecying terror

All this time later now he had held just so
The swing of her hair

Above such solid posture her teeth her mother's
Elegant familiar

More so than of late my own in the mirror
Vista of disclaim

Such agonies being young fanned in floods in flames
Of details like lost years:

'From time to time through all this
Sugaring dew-lapped

Rough fur thick pillow
Milkweed bursts

Undeterred psychotropic sutured
Sun's patchwork

Blistering drought receded harvest's
Skin graft

On the one hand Give me some sugar
Gettheebehindme

On the other   two days more no
Food no water

Breath in the mind overheated
Thought overheard

Of late skin holding fast   all I am
Is alive' —

At a glance lie down and sleep
And I'll talk now you

Yet I can't stop my ears my dears
Wide open the least

Wave parts this strange mechanic
Air of whatever

Love is   nothing past
Not ever

LOUD TALK IN THE OVERLIGHTED HOUSE

Those who have come by car from rumor to park
And park for free wherever there are no meters to pay
Then finding lights out cars gone empty porch
To sit awhile to smoke let the high wear out

Or to watch the hollow-hearted moon through trees
While a few drives down from another field of loss
Refugees laugh out loud over the river
Of street lamps and shelter and homeland securities

All without knowing for sure what could be lost
Hearing what they can't see in the lines of cable
Voyeurs' ears in a universe parallel
An eye on the window with the broken lock

An ear to the ground nights when strangers together
Gather themselves in the still pervading feel
Of perspectives leading somewhere else
Perpetual sound in the dark some reasoning will

— *What we don't know might hurt*—they listen for
Fearing the failure to carry to term—
Or worse carry out whatever was asked—
Or worse the success of becoming her

Gone from our lives forever and ever
Saddled with house we will never sell
For a profit that keeps us in mind afloat
In the cloudy glinting gutter water

Eyed from a raft so far from any other—
The four-eyed mirror of theirs and ours
The stagecoach and gun the long arm the kerchief
Once entertaining like no other chatter

Back at the guileless gut of the OK Corral
When doors were barred from sun up to high noon
High noon to sun down and the ghostriders came
And blew right through us in our bleacher seats

As we drew our breaths and our guns

KLANGFORBENMELODIE

"Our realization of what can happen
Has happened and over and over again
The field of ambition looks like the field of chance
One tall electrostatic rose and a nuclear plant
Having migrated upstate logged now on a map
With the Centers for Disease Control

What they'd thought was a good is a danger in fact
The niche they'd conceived inventive as all get-out
Thoreau in a greenwood paddling grown
Sun-crowded more selective than once it was
Nothing coming of solitude but a blinding black
Abundant under Hell's green mountains' shadows
The Past descendant from under the clouds
The paddle's bright atoms drop't to the plane of attack
Indivisible water returned to the wave —
Original beeloud glade heart's core bald street—

Each higher form ceasefire blank ruin of praise . . .
Bare ruined choirs' elite ignition of trees
Selective services as olive-branched
Texts drop't slow their seeds — any child knows this —
Igniting delight's base proteins binding their faults
In paradox and hierarchies of change
A terrible beauty broken by words —

But what's variable in lines of verse conceived
Cannot in life support the feint of return
To a pattern of indeterminate chance recurrence—

Each syllable that resists they say may double
The odds of progress true yet a poem feeds no one"

"SOUL IS THE BODY'S DREAM OF ETERNITY"

Why the poem and not the soul
As subject to this day's thought or music–dream
Why the made and not the unmade thing
Making a closed form in the close at least —
That the poem preclude such discourse or thinking
That the poem promise expertise
That the poem allow convention to spring
From torn-apart allegiances — not I
But the poem's evasive self-subjecting . . .

Abased at one remove to its bell of always
From anonymous voices one loves compassion placed
Snagged for a time on this performance speed
Another time and place researched
By tender sons and daughters of choice

First objects to I am . . .

Poem said all this . . .

Neither touch me nor survive me, said my Soul . . .

HEAT WAVE

Brown light gray clouds white boats
Flat thumbs of 10 raindrops
Respite yawn the Captain quoted said
This vessel's a regular Versailles
In a gust now those who sank interred
Rescued among shadow ducks and swans

Sunstroke flash flood guillotine
Firehouse on fire mechanical whine
The EMTs administered on site
Advil valium morphine
Up the block a shiver of fountain lights
Youth's hope stars' clarities

At times as now a fire a barge
Of misdirections a barrage of smoke
Three legs at night still to a crawl
Of last year the present present I recall
Calls off the volunteers till dawn

Oh Sphinx I remember nights like this
The high production feel we're paying for
Borderland and desert sweat
Frisson a toxin not ours theirs
A circus jest all right all night
Cutting a new well West awash
Across a floor that isn't any more
Though once it was a very likeness rich
And oozing charm from every pore
As it oiled its way to the blacktop saying,
"Symptoms are not Causes"

HEMLOCK

Dark night stole arrows of fortune's green

With one step sap laddered rain

Blood guttering in the scheme of things

A slow proceeding underfoot

Gleaming boughs' intense seeming felled

Dark acid of understanding keen

A finger cut on the dream of a map

Blood on the seam before world draws in

On the globed sphere of a child's nowhere

Curtains draw back at birth on awe

On metaphor and disbelief

Most beautiful when least seen

Perceiving nights and days that turn on each other

Lake steeled for more rain

To survive my love for a moment soft:

This ruthless hemlock

YELLOW TENNIS BALL

When the snowmelt passes
In the mudtracks there's left
Netsfull strained pulp
Last gasp trout speckled
Tone mud flats flow
Flux dream bed once
Dog ridden soft browed
Post June open mouthed
After lowlit dropshot
After backboard echo
Dimmed indoor solo
Coupled hit after hit
Uncrated on bedrest
Back tape fore court
Strong armed sudden death
Come on! shout childish

Winter pane water palace
Sun-yellow brains endless
Bronze ice rebound drain
Loud water-drops words ice
Swords unmoored leg carpark
Snowbank dog's mudtake
Trash handcart shed dark
River hose brown spade
Cloud tennis shod shot
Basket dragged takes cold
Pack plant fetch soil
Fertilize old high ways
Redbuds blurred black concrete
Wind stun power branched
Grey nest blue hunger
Blackout fetch sun lob

Unturned leaves come on now
Lost ball seed all last
From rose all dust things
Hit fall dust returns
Blue eyed sex storm
Of love heat's old
Year one oh Lord
Of love hit hit again
Hit hit hit returned

CORNER HOUSE

Of course the angles
The straight man
Straight backed

From Virginia the felon's
Cousins the last
Possessions a wake

Dawn's sympathetic yellow dishes stacked
The odds against another
Streetcorner duel

*

Look out
Through the lace
The tiny cracks in the glassine

Counteract
All too transparent peering
With cellphones the young

Add a year or two they think
But the corner faces
Decades   On the brink

Of being seen she dials
911 — a bottle in the neck
Who can blame her then?

*

Turns out everyone
When the next day comes
Not an egg or two

Not one if by land
A shot heard round the streets
A lot of work the realtor says

For all the fine details
And the well-made bed
Time's retributions are foregone

Not everyone's dream conforms
To a corner house —
Built-ins in the corner rooms —

A table leaf —

A shipwright's dream of
The afterlife

LAY THEM OUT IN LAVENDAR

Come in too fast and you'll stove in
Your pipe dreamed hat too slow
And the misunderstood
Among docksitters sunbathers travellers will
Becalm you too far
Offshore to swim
Oh Evolution

Dive in and you'll drown
A minute at the elbow
Of 103 North and 103A
At the lake's south end

In the clouds that break
A wealth of voices across water
Cutting past idle to moor
Where some farsighted Town
Official laid out the law
To bring in the exile

Mountains' genius by contrast lays
A path on the water beneath you itself

Ahead a flag   Shore sheds
Where once docked cows
Come home to heaven
The whole lake rimmed
With yellow and the oak

Time dropping
The future like flies

Faster than you'll say sawblade

Niche did you await
Me under a beech I meant
Only to lie down by
Its brother winter tore down
In whose blasted
Arms it's hung all spring
Crying Mercy Uncle

Had I a thousand sightlines
Back to branch the woods
Had given me
Water for an eye
Flies at carrion and mud
A leafchoked culvert

An eye for an eye
A vote for a vote is a myth
Of control that has the whiff
Of lavender
Shellacking them on that hill
Shelling them back to kingdom come
Laying them out
In firebugs flogging their plan

Can't we all get along
Said the beaten man
As wind blew back on his oar
And his cry grew up
To the roar of a man
In the wind's roar at nightfall
No one could ever hear ever
Never knowing whatever he knew
Nor that he would be   ever himself
Remembered

LAKE MIRROR

The mix of sun and clouds
Becomes a low near 67
A backlash stirring
A red tea parts

Regarding western cities
A backroutes's been hatched
The trail closely watched
Each car is a catchphrase caught

The trial that is sets out
To a graduate degree
A plain truth belaying
Recovery

At public.org I meant
1,100 raised/saved
Stimulus Acts raise
Deficits – true or false?

RHODODENDRON

Of the socket that does not let go
Every week past bloom
Through the leafwhorl now
Given to replicating

Each branch putting out
A white explosive pink
Another gorgeous palm
Sticky gums for the fortune lady

Cut down taken in stems sunk
To the midthigh coupled in vases
Meniscus-wound
A day a week a month

If anything grown a darker green
In fact more fleshly alive
Than torturously gone
Nothing more to hope to live to see

No still life like the pear tree's
Trenched through artillery
Felled between cousins
Milled on a farm in France

No sweat through an insult of Time
Though a lifetime spans
Rich soil's improbable odds
A front come together at mealtimes

Sun across shade
In the blue spruce tree
Blistered bloodsport of hawks
Growing tireless afternoons

A graffito of pasttimes
Knifed in the trunk
Love vaunteth not itself
War and *Peace*

FAMILY HOME

Then a red squirrel
Entered the front hall
Through a wall

And lived undetected
Leaving no track
Save a bottomless woven basket scrap

And the thought of his small
Clever scale clearly choreographed
For survival reminding us all

That the house still stands
However empty of facts
And asynchronous biased accounts

Of all those differences
And upheavals between first cause
And the consequence

Of the more than one way
To sink a nail lay
A pipe down for waste   restore

Or more questions of whether once one has been
One can ever (oh never!) again
Go without scripting a going back

In the same river twice
Of the flagstone's high gloss
Of Valspar's val oil

In which the black cat vanishes
As green as moss
Whenever the oil wears out and off

To reveal the natural stone
Whose gray-green matte
Lay giving a colder impression

First to last
As the cat unskinned squirrel
With the flat of his tail

MIRROR LAKE

True too is the dock most years
And June's inverted echo

Each plank a hill in a blue descent
As when we step on it

Underfoot the image of water and rock
The eye as it must must gauge between

The difference a kind of distance effect
And equals our sense

That others are here when we're not
Osprey loon heron

Whose voices thrown beyond appearances
Prove something iconic

Shades to us whose minds run in proofs:
Given time this plane

In the ear in the eye repeats
What has gone returns

Road staggering up into view
Having been pure moon

And beautiful
For making its point

WORLD TOO HOT TO STEP INTO

That boy
With electric clippers in his hand
Grown silvery small and pliable

Each window's waves
Of dimensional reds

Golds upended on shores
Green gravel lawn   A black sedan —

The hedge at his chest
The hedge at his feet here met

Meter's one quantity he can control

*

From the kitchen's yellow glare the king of rivers
From the front hall red blood drops with the dropping sun
From the living room flight of finches yellow gray doves
From his crown of thorns the rhododendron blooms
Bow to low pressure overhead

*

Outside
Power tools

And summer embalmed scentless
What suffers inside intangible promising joy

Nuclei profuse   ungovernable
Cascades of molecules he eyes

Formed on his tongue like bees to Ambrose his mark
Ownership   Exile   Some trees for poems

*

Between matter and sound the hour exchanged
Soon changed to cold dark

 All things whom shaking fastens more as real

His face where the streetlight faces gone
From both sides of the glass
When the light goes out

Then massed clouds

— for James Merrill

ACKNOWLEDGMENTS

Sections *iii, iv, and vi* of "Satires of Circumstance," in slightly different versions, were first published in *The Notre Dame Review, Winter, 2012.* "Cold War Free Radio" first appeared in *The New Yorker, May 25, 2015.* "Reading of Lebanon" was originally published in *Property* (Ausable/Copper Canyon, 2008). "Reading the Great War" first appeared in *The Yale Review,* Volume 95 Issue 3, 2007, and subsequently in *Property* (Ausable/Copper Canyon, 2008). Grateful thanks to the Editors and Publishers.

Deep gratitude to Stanley Moss, Christina Mengert, and Todd Portnowitz for sympathetic stewardship of this manuscript into print. Thank you James Richardson, Chase Twitchell, Marjorie Welish, Jane Shore, Howard Norman, David Michaelis, Ellen Tremper, for past and present conversation, hilarity, clarity, friendship, and encouragement. Love and thanks to Louise Kalin for your beautiful art, and to Louis Asekoff, friend, fellow, and colleague of the most generous heart.

BIOGRAPHICAL NOTE

JULIE AGOOS is the author of three previous collections of poems, *Property* (Ausable/Copper Canyon, 2008); *Calendar Year* (The Sheep Meadow Press, 1997); and *Above the Land* (Yale University Press, 1987), selected by James Merrill for The Yale Series of Younger Poets and winner of the Towson State University Prize for Literature. Recipient of the Grolier Poetry Prize, the Lloyd McKim Garrison Prize for Poetry from Harvard University, and a past Resident Fellow of The Frost Place, she coordinates the MFA Program in Poetry at Brooklyn College/CUNY, where she is Professor of English. She lives with her family in Nyack, NY.